Advance Praise for Maxim D. Shrayer's *Zion Square*

Maxim D. Shrayer's voice speaks across generations. With a stubborn belief that poetry must be healing, Shrayer writes poems that break through boundaries and fears, accept defeat, and yearn for pleasure. As morally serious and utterly sincere as these poems are, they are also filled with abhorrence, loathing, odium, and contempt. If humankind is to survive, Shrayer argues in this new collection, then it will do so with all the complexities of humankind: love, murder, kindness, torture, propaganda, and poetry.
—**David Biespiel**, author of *A Self-Portrait in the Year of the High Commission on Love*

"I have nothing to immolate/ except my memory/ but memory doesn't burn," so writes the Russian-born American Jew, scholar and translator, refusenik and son of refuseniks, poet and son of a poet, professor and student of life Maxim D. Shrayer. The memories he carries burn in carefully crafted verses as if to contain his furies and his love. Poems born since October 7, poems of Israel and the old Soviet Union, an imagination that can bring Nabokov to size up Putin, but can also relish the sweetness of concord grapes in Massachusetts. These are poems to savor and to learn.
—**Rodger Kamenetz**, author of *The Missing Jew: Poems 1976-2022*

Maxim D. Shrayer's *Zion Square* is a book of unabashed loyalties, outspoken in its political commitments, at moments bitingly satiric, at others, tender. The central question is one of home; at once diasporan and Zionist, the poems constantly seek the place where roving heart and mind can be at peace. Moving among the Eastern Europe of the poet's heritage and early life, cosmopolitan Western Europe, Boston and Cape Cod where he has put down roots, and Israel, his soul-home, the poems circle around an unease that contains the kernel of its own cure. "An immigrant Russian Jew/eager to live off his small property," Shrayer counts his blessings as the poems mingle hellos and goodbyes, sometimes paradoxically as what seemed past penetrates the present. An Old World melody, sweet, rueful, rises up above the ubiquitous rhetorical din of our moment.
—**Natania Rosenfeld**, author of *The Blue Bed*

Born in Moscow to a Jewish-Russian family with Ukrainian and Lithuanian roots, and a refusenik for more than eight years, Maxim D. Shrayer has lived a life containing much anguish. Still, his memorably polished verse in *Zion Square* gleams like the grapes in his poem "Grapes of Sukkot," that "shine upon us/ like our ancestors' desert stars." With carefully-observed details, Shrayer's poems summon up both history and its calamities as well as tender moments, as when the speaker in "Two Octaves for My Father" asks, "Remember, how the oak leaf spiraled,/ desperately, into mom's open hand?" Many of Shrayer's poems address, with desperation and despair, a world in painful conflict and chaos. Yet there is compassion in his poems, which tell us that the speaker has "nothing to immolate / except my memory" because "like a broken prayer/ memory won't leave the Jew alone." These haunted poems movingly try to make sense of our current world that is, Shrayer passionately reminds us, seeped in tragedy.
—**Yerra Sugarman**, author of *Aunt Bird*

Zion Square

Poems

Maxim D. Shrayer

Teaneck, New Jersey

ZION SQUARE ©2025 Maxim D. Shrayer. All rights reserved. No part of this book may be used or reproduced in any manner whatsoever without written permission except in the case of brief quotations embodied in critical articles and reviews.

Published by Ben Yehuda Press
122 Ayers Court #1B
Teaneck, NJ 07666

http://www.BenYehudaPress.com

To subscribe to our monthly book club and support independent Jewish publishing, visit https://www.patreon.com/BenYehudaPress

Jewish Poetry Project #57　　　　　　　　　　　　　　http://jpoetry.us

Ben Yehuda Press books may be purchased at a discount by synagogues, book clubs, and other institutions buying in bulk. For information, please email markets@BenYehudaPress.com

Cover image: Kikar Tsiyon, Jerusalem, May 2025, photo by Maxim D. Shrayer.

ISBN13 978-1-963475-71-5 pb

25 26 27 28 / 10 9 8 7 6 5 4 3 2 1　　　　　　　250710

In loving memory of my father,
David Shrayer-Petrov ז״ל

Contents

My Woven Kipa

The Ghost Trio / 2
Grapes of Sukkot / 6
My Woven Kipa / 7
UN General Assembly Resolution on Gaza / 8
Silentversities / 9
The Poets of Hamas / 10
Campus Confrontation / 11
Zion Square / 12

Verses about a Burned Passport

First Name and Patronymic / 16
Two Octaves for My Father / 17
Tallinn, April 1987 / 18
An Old Polish Poet in New England / 19
Delmonico / 21
How These Words of Love / 23
Verses about a Burned Passport / 24
The Soviet Rhetoric (After Mayakovsky) / 26
Anniversary / 27
Prediction / 28

Peculiarities of the National Pilgrimage

Our Fathers / 30
A Midsummer Night's Dream / 31
Last Will and Testament / 32
Another Day of War / 33
Victory Parade in Massachusetts / 34
Israeli Soldiers in Ukraine / 35
Peculiarities of the National Pilgrimage / 36
In Paris / 37
A Guide to Russian Vienna / 38
Benefactor / 39
Wine Tasting in Winter / 41
Mourning / 42

Afterword / 45
Acknowledgments / 46
About the author / 47

My Woven Kipa

The Ghost Trio

A Jewish organist is playing in a Black church
from the Russian of David Shrayer-Petrov

1. Allegro

Where, where is the ghost?
Whose is the ghostly presence?
What's hidden and what's lost?

The time has come for penance.
But there's no guilty party,
only a shimmering appearance.

All three musicians strive for clarity
of sound, for crisp and lucid phrasing—
but chamber music isn't charity.

And so they go on rehearsing,
Sunday after Sunday, the date
of their performance nearing.

Memorial Day already. Pollinate
and suffer. Boston suburbs choke.
Asthmatic coughing. Concentrate

on squiggly notes, music's secret joke.
And then the ghost will finally betray
its pallid face, its dagger and its cloak.

So many things we hesitate to say
come out when musicians play.

2. Largo

The violinist dons his Sunday garments,
he looks so dapper in the charcoal linen suit
and periwinkle shirt—his husband's present.

He takes a sip of pure water. Claims his seat
beside the piano, in a square of dusty light.
He wipes his brow, foreswearing the heat,

rosins his bow, myopically smiling at the cellist.
He dreams of taking a lukewarm lavender bath
at his apartment in the South End. The list

of fortunes goes on—the violinist's lucky path.
His surgeon husband. Summers on the Vineyard.
A named chair at Longy. Freedom from all the wrath,

resentment, anger. Only practiced love and gratitude
for what his parents, doctors who had met at Brown,
instilled in them—a sense of pride and also a shrewd

refusal to let their bodies become the battleground
of history—which doesn't mean the violinist was taught
to unremember kinsfolk in Montgomery and Richmond.

The violinist sighs and gives the cellist a thoughtful nod
as if to say: the pianist's always late. But we, we're on time.
He wants to compliment the cellist on her luscious red

hair arranged in a French braid, but such pantomime
of gender could be misconstrued. He holds the note,
observing quietly the cellist's dress, the color of lime,

her swiveling silver earrings, her ancient aquiline nose.
What does he know about her, the violinist wonders.
They have been playing for two years. Yes, those

bottomless blue eyes. What's buried in them? Others
on the Boston music circuit told him she cannot offend.
Her husband is some sort of Jewish poet. Figures

he must be a professor. That's how American artists mend
their budgets. The violinist strains to remember other facts:
the cellist's teenage daughters play varsity tennis. No end

Zion Square

to the suburban tedium he's been spared. The ornate face
of the clock grins at the violinist as he fidgets, recollecting
that a swastika was recently painted on the cellist's fence.

The pianist finally arrives. She's twenty minutes late. Sing-
song voice. Apologies. Caleb was running a fever. She left
her cell phone on the counter and had no way of getting

in touch. She's really sorry. In her wavy tie-dyed skirt
she looks a bit jejune, the violinist observes. She must
be strapped for cash, the cellist thinks, yet she has the spirit

to play despite her personal mishaps. The violinist and the cellist
both know the pianist is a mess. A divorcée. Three children. Debts.
A maze of private lessons. Living in her family's nest,

an old New England farmhouse, where her retired parents
obsess about their ancestors' Mayflower pedigree
and socialize with other Yankees from a museum of the past.

They start to play. Allegro laced with doubt, tinged with glee.
They're finally all together. Are they, though, are they?
The score commands performing it *vivace e con bri-*

o pianist, please don't overthink the music, just play
as written, the violinist whispers while the cellist notes
to herself that no matter what, she mustn't hold sway

over the trio lest the ghost suddenly decide to come out.
The largo starts. All three musicians know that the ghost
is somewhere nearby. Which ghost, though? And which route

will it take to break the silence? Whose misery does it host?
The ghost of racism, *con vibrato*, where's your entrance?
The ghost of Jew-hate, come. Next the ghost who is the most

camouflaged: white privilege. Whose past does it conceal?
Hushed tones of gentility. Whose pain do they reveal?

3. Presto

Their last rehearsal on the first Sunday in June.
They race though the allegro. Arpeggios of vengeance
still hovering like stormy clouds. A haunting tune

across the sooty sky over the suburbs. Innocence
is lost. They get through the allegro on pins and chords.
But at the largo things fall apart. Now the sentence.

What privilege? Where? the piano plaintively accords.
What racism? You don't know? the violin tremulates.
What Jew-hatred? Stop pretending! the cello soars.

Please. You're both made of whiteness, sings the violin.
White privilege, white bread, white lies, intones the pianist.
Compare pain? I can't, the cellist rings. My father was in Buchenwald.

The black violinist halts and rests the violin on his knees.
The Jewish cellist awkwardly gets up and walks away in tears.
Only the pianist, only the white pianist pounds the keys.

The music rips the skein of being. The ghost is proudly silent.
A triumph of difference. Discordant and defiant.

Grapes of Sukkot

In the first spring of COVID fever,
still quarantined and fearful,
we bought a tall townhome
directly across the street
from Holyhood Cemetery,
where Rosemary Kennedy rests,
sidelined from world fame.

The Irish builder left us
with limelight hydrangeas,
two leggy black maples,
and a weeping cherry—
blossoming, useless to me,
an immigrant Russian Jew
eager to live off his small property.

I planted a Concord vine—
that local philosopher of grapes,
that simpleton of jelly flavor—
in the far corner of our V-shaped yard,
where mint and sage now scent the air
and Stella the silver Jewdle gallops,
hunting for rabbits and possums.

Three springs and three autumns hence
the vine has spread its veiny dactyls
across the sky and fence,
forming the panels of a tabernacle—
no longer portable but still transient,
and the clusters of grapes shine upon us
like our ancestors' desert stars.

My Woven Kipa

for Maxim Mussel

I bought my kipa
from an old mystic
who spends his days
at Shuk HaCarmel.

My kipa is woven
from many strands:
black like memory
of the 9th of Av,
blue like the eyes of
murdered Litvak maidens,
white like the linen shroud
I will wear to my burial,
coarse like salt
from the Dead Sea,
soft like the sand of the Negev,
silken like milk
of Bedouin camels.

My best childhood
friend from Moscow,
who lives north of Tel Aviv
in a rickety building
without a bomb shelter,
told me, "You've become
a religious Zionist,"
when we spoke
two or three days
after the Hamas attack
and I was seething
with useless words
of righteous rage.

I didn't want to argue.
My friend stood in the landing
by the window. Missiles were
flying across his phone screen.

UN General Assembly Resolution on Gaza

On Friday, October 27th, 2023:

120 countries voted in favor
(that is, against Israel).

14 countries voted against
(that is, 13 for Israel and Israel for herself).

45 countries abstained
(abstained).

Silentversities

silentversities	silently witness
silentversities	fail to condemn
silentversities	soulless and witless
silentversities	solo and in tandem
silentversities	hostile to Israel
silentversities	seek compromise
silentversities	toxic with vitriol
silentversities	breaking the promise
silentversities	charging tuition
silentversities	have no excuse
silentversities	failing their mission
silentversities	banishing Jews

The Poets of Hamas

for Franck Salameh

The poets of Hamas bemoan the death
of one of their own. Villanelles and sonnets
deny that men from Gaza violated Jewish girls
time and again, in gangs, with rabid zeal. They
call it Zionist "lies" and "smokescreens." Bloody rhymes
with bloody Jewish bodies. Terza rima
of mutilated babies, cut-off breasts,
heroic couplets, slender Gazan stanzas
by learned men who die to murder Jews.

In Boston and in London poets mourn
their fellow rhymesters. How they guzzle down
their martyred verse on X and Instagram,
their ghazals of ecstasy amid the rubble,
hamasaat of their chivalrous exploits
into Israeli farmland, *quasaa'id* to mark
the glorious advent of intifada, *maraathi*
where Israel always rhymes with death—
in London and in Boston poets spread this hatred.

Campus Confrontation

> *"What are you doing still awake?"*
> *She answered him:*
> *"I love."*
>   from the Russian of Leonid Martynov,
>   translated by Tatiana Rebecca Shrayer and Maxim D. Shrayer

"Are you a Zionist?" they asked,
their faces covered in keffiyehs.
On their chessboard hate was masked.
She stood alone. She had no fear.
"No Zionist can come inside
the library. Go back to Poland."
"From enemies I will not hide,"
she told them, stoically. And
she smiled at their virulence.
When they closed in, she clenched her fists
although she already knew
that rancor feeds on ignorance.
They asked, "Are you a Zionist?"
She answered: "Yes, I am a Jew."

Zion Square

> *A sixty-year-old smiling public man*
> Yeats

In the earthly city of Jerusalem I like to stay
just a couple of blocks from Kikar HaMusica
in Yo'el Moshe Salomon Street, a pathway
named after the founder of three Israeli towns
and a Hebrew newspaper, a descendant
of a messenger of the venerable Vilna Gaon,
who in the 1800s left Lithuania for the Holy Land,
and was, perhaps, my distant relative, or rather
kinsman on the side of my father's grandfather
Rabbi Chaim-Wolf, of blessed memory, who was
peacefully murdered in the early days of the war.

Orchestras played outside my hotel at night and
I listened to the music Jews couldn't leave in Europe.
I felt sheltered by the might of the Iron Dome
but also the roof of particolored umbrellas that
hang over the street—once the prey of tourist
photos and travel agents' brochures, now the sky
of our small warring country. I looked up and cried
for all my cousins-in-arms but also for myself. Mostly
tears of joy and comfort. Music didn't end suddenly,
it flowed up toward Jaffa Street and I felt someone
or something carry me, a Jewish feather, to Kikar Tsiyon.

Next morning, as I waited for my muse in uniform, I got
to observe a troop of teenage boys in woven kipot,
black and white Jews who danced in synch and looked
like pale versions of kids from an urban ghetto, vestiges
of another world, performing in support of hostages,
while girls in long skirts collected donations. Jerusalemites
stood and watched, tired of having to care, unfree to let
their war fatigue spoil the mood of unity. It was then,
weaving my way through a maze of men and women
toward the imaginary proscenium that separated
the dancers from the dance, I saw a vision of the past.

Or was it a vision of the future? I still don't know.
I can only tell you what it looked like: Head to toe,
hat to shoes, spectacles to trousers, above and below,
black kipa, black kapote, black gartel—meant to separate
heart from sex organs—it was all there to reincarnate
what I thought my Litvak ancestors had left behind.
He was neither tall nor short, neither skinny nor rotund,
both redhead and whitehead, eyes both blue and hazel,
tousled hair, unevenly clipped beard, blackened fingers,
hands in flight, conducting the performance of the universe.
Who was he, a local shtetl fool or G-d to all his Jews?

Verses about a Burned Passport

First Name and Patronymic

Nabokov travels to the Kremlin—
to visit Putin at his office,
he giggles awkwardly, he cringes
and lights a cigarette. The face
of Russia's ruler he examines
while blowing out purple smoke.
He quickly notes the ferret features,
the smile of a petty rogue.

Barely containing his repulsion—
aristocrat, aesthete, contrarian—
Nabokov slowly says to Putin:
"Your luck is over, you ruffian.
I'm taking back what's mine forever:
my father's name, my patronymic.
From now on you're 'putinvova,'
From now on you're doomed to vanish."

Two Octaves for My Father

Dad, do you remember, a frenzied
doe dashed across the clearing
and vanished, leaving behind the odor
of time—sharp, anguished?
We stood in silence as the echo carried
the cranes of exile: shrieking blares.
The grass was tall and wet, the sky was clear,
you drew a Star of David in the air.

Remember, how the oak leaf spiraled,
desperately, into mom's open hand?
The blazing yellow, the red, the autumn sprawled
across the woods and took the gasping land.
Split pine trunks were shaped like weather-beaten
harps that captive Hebrews wouldn't play.
For the refusenik years, the stolen ones,
O Russia, daughter of Babylon

Tallinn, April 1987

We were drinking in a pub,
taking random words apart
to find meaning.
Hurrying like a human soul
Baltic rain splashed the street
with longing.

Dark-green absinthe
breathing conifer, mint
and wormwood.
The wind howled a foxtrot
without sparing the notes
of brooding.

We left behind our table
where empty tumblers tremble
with boredom.
Lime trees lining the thoroughfare
spread their branches into the air
like bare arms.

An Old Polish Poet in New England

> *Unintelligible absolution and an end*
> Wallace Stevens

> *in memoriam Genrikh Sapgir*

Clutching
      Paschal tulips
            under his
                  right arm.
She, the chosen one? Tulle shivering
geraniums shriveling on hoar-frosted
windowsills. Passion's frozen ledge.

Have I misjudged?
It happened once before,
a summerly suburb of Kraków,
tail-curled drakes, raspy love calls
summoning hens over
blooming ponds and cemeteries
crammed with
broken
      Jewish
           graves.

On that day the father of my *kochanie*,
a bone-dry fanatic, spoke to me
from his creaky porch:
"My holy daughter Sarah
will never be given to a lover
of eel and suet!"

And
      I swore:
           a Jewess
                never again.

Swaying elm trees on Chapel Street.
Two drifters smoking at the corner.
A mounted cop in slow motion.
The poet is nervous. English sounds
romp down the clayish street and thump.

Why
        does
                the stupid heart
                              still pound?

Now finally her building.
A third-floor walkup.
Greasy stairs. The door ajar.
A Polish movie poster on the wall.

In the kitchen:

elder,
        beard,
                sidelocks,
sits,
        black coat,
                beanie,
rips
        his shirt
                and
bangs
        his
                bony
head
        against
                the table.

Maxim D. Shrayer

Delmonico

> *Now as I was young and easy under the apple boughs*
> Dylan Thomas

There was a time
I used to play pilgrim
in New Haven colony
where I lived just a block
from the theological seminary
and I walked valorously
to a neighborhood grocery
on Orange Street
where on Friday afternoons
tenebrous Italian wives
would buy Delmonico steaks
for their husbands.

I, too, would order
a Delmonico steak
and the name of it sounded
so triumphantly American,
auguring a new home,
promising to correct
each and every mistake
a greenhorn makes.

I've since forgotten
the face of the butcher
and the dress of the grocer's wife,
yet I still remember
the old Calabrian man
in shirtsleeves, black trousers
and railroad suspenders,
who had founded the business
back in the 1940s and now stood
at the helm of the cash register
and packed brown bags
with his tremorous hands…

He must have detected
something European
in the way I conducted myself
or in the way I pronounced
the word *Delmonico*—
like a nobleman's name.
Where you come from?
he would ask,
first in English,
then in Italian
each time he saw me,
Di dove sei? Di dove sei?

And each time he asked
I would answer, eagerly,
Nato in Russia,
the streetspun Italian
I had picked up in Ladispoli
as a twenty-year-old
Jewish kid from Moscow
waiting for my refugee visa.

In those New Haven days
of immigrant innocence
I would walk back to my garret
under the oaks and Victorian turrets
and so acutely, so strongly I felt
the daily charms of belonging
as I whispered *o Delmonico, my Delmonico…*
How little remains
of that fleshy moniker—
only deracinated sounds
laced with dull pain
of the American dream.

How These Words of Love

for K.

A film of ochre on the leaves
and on the breath a scent of red wine—
this is the way the autumn feels
when it has mixed gold and carmine
and drawn into the lungs, no: gills
the mystical October salts.

Why gills—is it a glittery carp?
A catfish fattened on feasts of summer?
The words are random, in the park
I plucked them from the ground on Sunday,
I bought them at the corner store,
I heard them once. I have restored

their sound in your native tongue.
My only one, please understand:
I used to hear them all the time
in Russian. Then a muteness and
a wordlessness. Years of silence.
No rhymes, no meters; a suspense.

I kept imagining them in my head
without hearing them in English.
My Russian poems weren't dead,
I wanted you to feel them tingling.
And finally… Today, we took
a morning walk, you wore a coat

of weightless wool, the maple leaves
were rustling underfoot, the runners
were flitting by, Canada geese
flocked to the soccer field, forerunners
of early winter. You removed your gloves,
You kissed me. How these words of love?

Verses about a Burned Passport

A Berlin-based artist,
born in Bukhara
to a family of former evacuees
and raised in Brooklyn
in the midst of Soviet émigrés,
burned his Russian passport
in front of a small crowd
on Unter den Linden.

At the opening of an anti-war installation
an inquisitive German journalist
posed a question to the artist:
"I thought you were Ukrainian—
where did the Russian passport come from?
And why burn it?"

The author of the burned passport
replied to the German:
"I'm an American expat Jew
of Ukrainian descent.
My Russian passport
is nothing but an error of history.

"My ancestors hail from outside Kharkiv.
And only one grandmother
is Russian, but actually
a Chuvash, a Cheremissian,
an old Soviet chameleon…
enough already with
your silly questions!
It was an act of protest
against atrocities.
An act of self-purification."

I read this account on social media
and thought to myself:
"They took away my Soviet passport
at the time of emigration
in exchange for an exit visa to Israel,
which was subsequently stolen
in Pompeii at the Temple of Fortuna Augusta
and later replaced with
Italian refugee papers—
I showed them when entering America."

I have nothing to immolate
except my memory
but memory doesn't burn
at the Brandenburg Gate
in the shadow of flowering lime trees
on Unter den Linden
on the banks of the Spree
like a broken prayer
memory wouldn't leave the Jew alone.

The Soviet Rhetoric (After Mayakovsky)

A Russian immigrant once asked Ilhan Omar:
"O Congresswoman, do you have to mar
all things Israeli? Your wrathful tweets
elude a balanced view of the Near East."

His pleas ignored, a Russian immigrant then turned
to the elected whipper-tweeter from Detroit:
"I want to know, Representative Tlaib,
do you rehearse or is it all *ad lib?*"

No answer followed. A Russian immigrant
still had a lingering hope the Squad would grant
his wish: "Please, Representative Ocasio-Cortez,
give Israel another fighting chance."

And only Bernie Sanders knew their ruse:
That Soviet rhetoric works better than the truth.

Anniversary

in memoriam Louise Glück

Some artists die in peace. No such luck
for the American poet who nearly shared
her Jewish-Hungarian name with Maestro Gluck,

he, to whom a young genius was once compared
favorably. Lethean music has since lapped
over the maestro's name, while Amadeus has fared

well in the waters of oblivion. Wild flowers, trapped
in her painterly verse, are now free to bloom and wither,
except the tall blue iris of her face. Untapped

secrets of her craft will go with her or dither
on the brink of time. Such is the destiny of art.
I remember a poetry reading in Cambridge. The weather,

wretched. Robert Pinsky, David Ferry, and Frank Bidart,
known locally as the "poem doctor," all reading by her side,
like aging knights still trying to win her heart.

At the end, after waiting for the admirers to subside,
I came up. What could I say that she didn't already know—
so perfectly beautiful, lonely, hazel-eyed?

About her turns of verb that glut and glow—
refusing to grow weary of their own poetry
yet surrendering to the universal undertow?

I said, "Ms. Glück, I love your poem 'Anniversary.'"
"Which one?" she asked. "I have written two already."

Prediction

for Rodger Kamenetz

The year we married
my late father-in-law,
who as a child
had survived Transnistria,
told my wife that

I would be a noose
around her neck and
all I would want to do
is stay at home
and write poems.

He was wrong
about poverty
and the noose,
but he was right
on the nose
about poetry.

Peculiarities of the National Pilgrimage

Our Fathers

for Fedor Poljakov

How did our fathers survive so many decades of Soviet mendacity?
How did they manage to teach us the antidote to memory?
There lived in them such an elegant Jewish audacity:

how deftly they sidestepped the rules of cruel history,
how they tied the knots of their silk neckties a little askance,
disliked hollow words, stains on the tablecloth, unpolished cutlery,

how they forgave the cowardice of colleagues and despised laziness,
how gorgeously they pronounced "a punch in the mouth" or "knock 'em dead,"
and how they hated holidays with bread and games and impure language.

After a father's departure an empty trench remains in one's head…
Our dear soldiers are done fighting, curing the sick, rhyming, singing,
and I don't know how to put it without oversimplification. Instead

one evening in June you and I will find ourselves in front of Retsina Café,
after traversing Judenplatz, once the center of Jewish life, now an emptiness.
We'll go inside, feel the aroma of resinated wine and see the carefree fa-

ces of the Viennese who don't know guilt. We'll occupy a table beneath the vistas
of Naxos and remember our fathers after the Russian, Jewish, and Byzantine rites.
Then we'll go downstairs into the past, where they are eighteen and the muses

wear black narrow skirts, where filterless cigarettes burn like streetlights;
where tears are formally banned and sons not allowed to sulk,
only to play Biriba and laugh; where grim merrymakers sit around in black vests;

where on the kitchen counter in a deep dish sleeps the coarse Levantine salt,
where, panting, lie the three fish of sorrow: sea bream, flounder, and red mullet.

A Midsummer Night's Dream

for K.

At slumbertime I usually wander
across the internet (the everlasting poison),
when I come up to the bedroom,
you're asleep, and on my pillow, to the right of
your head, guarding your peace,
lies our miniature poodle, Stella;
before hiding myself in your solace
I move her over with my arm and shoulder.

At first our poodle barely stirs,
only her fine long curls sparkle
in the dark, her phosphorescent
head showing blackened silver.
Then she jumps off and drinks for a long time
from a glistening enamel vessel,
and falling into the binding of dreams,
I hear sounds of simple-hearted mysticism.

At dawn, when all the Eastern Phoebes
are done fainting, and the Doves done mourning,
when in the double harness of the nebulae
a chariot rides over the morning horizon,
at the boundary of darkness and daybreak,
the intersection of life and deathlessness,
I really don't want you to awaken,
don't go yet, when else we'll be together...

Last Will and Testament

Thomas Mann has returned to the city of Lübeck.
The municipal elders have gathered to welcome him home.
He's old. He blushes. He feels like a young German lover.
And he doesn't know how to abolish his shame.

Katia Mann tells her husband: "We don't belong in this country.
How eerie this place, how sated with murderous joy.
All is lost. At the *Kirche* the bride has been wailing since sunrise.
Buxtehude's great organ has been vandalized and destroyed."

"Darling," says Thomas Mann. "On the strand of my youth, Travemünde,
sand is weightless like ashes and cold like unearthly embrace.
All my life I've been faithful to Germany. Now what an ending
to discover that nothing of mine remains."

Another Day of War

I fold my laptop, leash
my silver poodle and leave
for work—to give a lecture
about Primo Levi's death.

We traverse the neighborhood
where Boston Brahmins once lived.
Bleeding lancets stir under our feet
as I revise a ditty from my childhood:

Children ran into the house,
mad with joy on Christmas eve,
there is no harmony, alas,
and there is no place for Jews.

Victory Parade in Massachusetts

A Soviet immigrant is going to war.
Well, if not war then a battle for the past…
Shuffling her shattered shoes across Harvard Square
she might as well be getting ready to land on Mars.
The old woman was only twenty-two during the victorious spring,
and she's still grateful, parading her wits and wares.

She remembers August 1941, the Red Cavalry brigades
destroyed by panzers. Her grandparents, parents, younger siblings,
their whole mishpocha murdered at Kamianets-Podilskyi. Then
December outside Moscow, the ripped field wire of the division HQ,
she held it in her teeth all night, never recovering from the order,
"Not a Step Back," terrified that the Germans would get through.

A Jewish corporal, she was recommended for a Red Star, but she only
got copper pennies, how they clickety-clack like streetcars,
a Medal for Valor, and four other medals over four years of the war,
today they ring hollow and jangle like other people's tales,
now exploding with her broken-English despair,
now screeching in her desiccated Russian larynx.

Mummy dearest, where are you going? This isn't the right
time, her Dnipro-born prudent daughters implore her,
both of them suburban American Jews in their sixties.
When right time, my dear children? What I fight for?
So now I must unfasten and take off holster
of memory? So I forget everything? Stay silent like coward?

Mummy, that was then, and this is now… But the specter
of the old Soviet woman grimly marches off to war
for the perfect past. Or is it a war with the past perfect?
No one, immigrant or native, has won such a battle before.

Israeli Soldiers in Ukraine

Israeli soldiers volunteering in Ukraine,
your Ukrainian accents audible in Russian
but not in Hebrew. Your faces Levantine,
your Stars of David like insignia of pain.

Israeli soldiers fighting in Ukraine,
at Soledar and Bakhmut, Mariupol and Kherson,
in fields of ripening wheat, in valleys of stone,
in seething trenches and open terrain.

Israeli soldiers dying for Ukraine,
where your ancestors lie in ditches and ravines,
could you imagine a Ukrainian bard
or poet crying for Gaza but not for Israel?

Peculiarities of the National Pilgrimage

Old virile German men and women come to the Holy Land in early November, warm their bones at the edge of the Dead Sea, admire Jacques Offenbach at the Israeli Opera, and sigh with bravura over their long lost youth right at the entrance to Yad Vashem.

Old sentimental Austrian men and women come to the Holy Land in the middle of April, sip cloudy cappuccinos at Landwer Café, founded by Viennese refugees, unveil their bulging veins on Bograshov Beach at noon, buy cheap antiquities at the flea market in Old Jaffa.

Old Jewish-Russian men and women don't come to the Holy Land in the fall or the spring, don't drink bitter vodka at Viking Restaurant on Ben Yehuda, don't listen to runaway poets at Babel Bookstore on Allenby, don't drag their heavy feet over the pouty stones of Jerusalem,

because old Russian men and women have already died or haven't yet been resurrected, because old Jewish men and women have already been resurrected or haven't yet died.

In Paris

An American woman is riding pillion
with her young French lover.
Fumes hover along the Seine.

With a careless gesture
the woman tosses into the river
a cigarette butt charged with her

spectral scent. She misses, barely
noticing the purple winged rats
attacking the blood-marked

object. Roofs are on fire, hands
teeter in garrets, booksellers'
ragged corduroy jackets stand

before her eyes. A back-breaking
sonorous wind trembles on her lips.
Bending down to her knees to

straighten the hem of her long
skirt, she screams out to her lover:
"Please hurry, my darling,

please speed up, we must
overtake this merciless sunset."

A Guide to Russian Vienna

Now put the cash away, conniver,
this gets you nowhere *in Wien*.
Jump in the Uber, tell the driver
you want to go back to Lviv.

The driver from Chechnya or Georgia
will recognize your cheap burlesque.
A refugee? Like hell you are,
colonial hunger in your eyes.

Ukrainian fricatives have trouble
exploding in your Nevan throat.
They called your bluff. They pierced your bubble.
You're nobody but yourself.

Freud's favorite analyst. A leading
supporter of Secession.
A firebird born of Soviet legends,
Empire's useful idiot.

Forget your past. It's worth deleting:
the savage war, the awkward rhyme.
Transform yourself and start believing
in your inexpiable crime.

Benefactor

> *in memoriam Ilia Salita*

Soundlessly you enter the most foreign of my dreams,
clutching under your left arm a cognac leather briefcase,
in which two choral synagogues would simultaneously fit.

You invite me to lecture before veterans of the great
patriotic war about any appropriate topic I didn't make up,
for instance: Botvinnik's chess, Oistrakh's agile fingers,

Golda Meir's endless cigarettes, Vasily Grossman's lovers,
Trumpeldor's last words, Moshe Kutuzov's glass eye,
Brodsky's salad-green Mercedes, Sergey Brin's birthplace.

I agree on the spot. The terms, very lucrative: business class,
conference at Yad Vashem, survivors' caustic whispers,
your baggy double-breasted suit, opening remarks about love.

We trade the usual pleasantries, wives and kids, the sun's
already setting over Moscow or Boston, Tel-Aviv or Berlin.
Well, it all makes sense, you say in that coarse falsetto,

nonfiction, fiction, now a screenplay, surely you should do it,
and we'll support, but in the film Russian Jews must appear.
Perhaps, disappear? I make a joke. Wouldn't it be great to write

a script about a Jewish Oblomov? In your eyes of a Moscow wunderkind
endless streams of heavy trucks flow on the Leningrad Highway.
The chocolate liquor of our Brezhnevian youth... In America we've grown

different. And yet, each time we meet, a hanging bridge ties itself
to our past, where alternative laws of gravitation and attraction rule, where
we walk from the sciences building to the main tower of Moscow State.

December outdoors. Sheepskin coat, fur hat, a vile mohair scarf,
for some reason you're telling me, a poet's son, about poets who
fought the Germans—Slutsky, Levitansky, Samoilov, Mezhirov, Vinokurov—

haven't I seen them all in person, live at the Writers House?
But I wouldn't include the last one, donut with dogshit as he was
(I repeat what I once heard as a kid on the train from Vilnius to Moscow

in a drunken conversation of littérateurs who translated from the Lithuanian
into the language of the Empire, but that's probably too hard
to interpret). Meanwhile you and I hurry to join a weightlifting club

under the direction of Robert Roman, son of a Latvian Rifleman. They accept
you but reject me. They reject you when I try to introduce you to my Beatles-
loving friends. They nominate you to join the school's Komsomol committee,

and me, the son of refuseniks, they try to throw out of the university.
But now all of this has lost not only its meaning but also its form,
the perfumed smoke of our student years has long since lifted.

We sit at a table in a French pastry shop, you have only twenty
minutes before your next meeting. From your chest cavity you take out
three tablets at once: for notetaking, for headaches, and one more,

which resembles the one Moses was given, and also a hungry pelican,
and a watchman at an old Jewish cemetery. You look terribly tired,
in your cloudy eyes of a mortally wounded gazelle I see cascading

reflections: everything we once considered alien but loved the way
our people loved their rotgut, their Russian wives, their enemies.
Did you finish the screenplay? you ask me, slowly. Isn't it about time?

I take a sip of my black coffee. I take a bite of my cheese Danish.
What can I tell you? Thank you, benefactor mine, but unfortunately
I cannot finish this script. Everything that we once shared, considered

our very own has become alien, and it no longer aches. You see,
benefactor, first the war on the land where our grandparents were born,
then another war on the land where we would like to find eternal rest.

What kind of a Jewish-Russian script can I compose today? What kind
of a funeral wailing song? Please forgive me, I just couldn't let you down.

Wine Tasting in Winter

At a wine tasting outside San Gimignano I met
a Saudi aristocrat with perfectly chiseled fingers.
His noble face was stuck half the distance
between Rabbi Marx's and Rabbi Freud's,
but swarthier. Together we stood on a grassy
terrace overlooking fourteen terracotta towers,
a sloping vineyard, and a mound of silver olive trees.
I said the world had gone mad, and he understood
I didn't mean it to be about the war but only about
the summer sun of Tuscany on that February afternoon.

He was sipping Chianti with a faint peppery nose.
I was wearing a dark blue kipa with a white trim.
The Saudi said he and his friend were driving to Milan
for a soccer game, and I said they were so lucky.
Come with us, he offered, we have two extra tickets.
I was tempted to say thank you, *akhi*, but I held back.
He looked away and tugged at his smoldering beard
as I retreated and returned to my table, my wife
and younger daughter, and my unfinished crostata
made of flour, sugar, butter, and blood orange.

Mourning

My generous father, a myopic Jewish boxer,
lies buried in a suburb west of Boston.

His parents sleep in what was once called Leningrad.
I used to visit them before the outbreak of COVID.

Two years later Putin's troops were sent to kill Ukraine;
I gave up hope of going back to Russia—once again.

Which in a way could be an immigrant's blessing:
to bury one's dead where one's children will go on living.

The irony is sweet: his cemetery's called American Friendship.
Some of my father's neighbors came to Ellis Island on a ship.

I've walked around his block, I've stood under a giant oak,
and I have yet to find a single Russian Jew or a refusenik.

My father, a New England poet by choice and by persuasion,
rests in the neighborhood of Jewish trades for all occasions.

I bring him round pebbles, place them on the sagging loam.
There's no gravestone yet. We'll give his body time to settle in.

We'll give it time because I, too, will need more time to finish
the curve of grief. It's taken me a while to say in English

or to whisper it in Russian: He's gone. He's physically gone.
My father won't go fishing with me or read my poems. Alone

I'm bound to fail where the two of us used to be so eloquent.
Yet I still wake up every day attempting an experiment.

And is it any consolation to know that time is lenient
with those who refuse to give up hope of a reunion?

I know my father is alive. There's no end to lineage,
as long as there's memory and universal language.

Afterword

This is a book of war, love, despair, and mourning.

War continues to rage in Ukraine, the birthland of my grandfathers and maternal grandmother.

The terror attacks of October 7 plunged Israel, the homeland of my heart, into another war. I have been going to bed with hopes of peace and justice and waking up to more news of violence and abandonment. No wonder then that war and confrontation have been on my mind, and much of my recent writing output has been focused on Ukraine and Israel and on disentangling from my Russian—Soviet—past.

In writing parts of this book, I have refused to rely on "people's tales [and…] printed columns of news," as one of my literary heroes, the poet and Shoah witness Ilya Selvinsky, put it in a poem of 1942. I wanted to let my inner eyewitness do the work of observing and understanding.

The bulk of the poems gathered under these covers was composed after October 7. The collection took its final shape after a trip to Israel in May 2024, during which I traveled up and down the country, lectured and gave readings, saw lots of family and friends, and even picked apricots and plums in the company of a fellow Jewish writer who had made *aliyah*.

My father, David Shrayer-Petrov ז״ל, died in Boston on 9 June 2024. He is in many verses of this book, and I dedicate it to his memory.

M.D.S.
December 2024

Acknowledgments

This book would not exist, either in its Russian and Jewish origins or in its Anglo-American shape, were it not for my late father, David Shrayer-Petrov, who taught me poetry, and my mother, Emilia Shrayer, who taught me English.

And this book would never have been composed without the love and support of my wife, Karen E. Lasser, and our daughters, Tatiana Rebecca Shrayer and Mira Isabella Shrayer. And Stella's polymetric barks are in many of these rhythms.

Twice-removed previous Russian incarnations of four poems included here first appeared in my collections *Tabun nad lugom* (Herd above the Meadow), *Amerikanskii romans* (American Romance), and *N'iukheivenskie sonety* (New Haven Sonnets). Earlier and much earlier versions of some of the poems appeared in the following journals and magazines: *arc 31: Journal of the Israel Association of Writers in English, Balagan, Blue Mountain Review, Green Golem: The Zionist Literary Magazine, Iron Words: Israel War Stories, Jewish Journal of Los Angeles, Judith Magazine, Massachusetts Bard Poetry Anthology 2024, Of The Book, Proof of Life: An Anthology, ROAR (Russian Oppositional Arts Review), Samfiftyfour, Vita Poetica,* and *Writing on the Wall.* Parallel Russian versions of some of these poems have appeared in the magazines *Artikl'* (Israel), *Novyi zhurnal* (New York), *Novyi svet* (Toronto), and *ROAR* (Israel). I would like to thank the editors and staff for having given e-space and print-space to my work.

Dobrochna Fire read and critiqued an early version of the manuscript with her usual tact and tolerance for my translingual quirks.

Julia Knobloch, who curates the Ben Yehuda Press Poetry Project, selected my book for publication and offered many constructive suggestions as she prepared the manuscript for publication. I am most grateful to her and to Larry Yudelson and Julie Sugar, publisher and associate publisher of Ben Yehuda Press, for giving my collection a hospitable home.

About the author

Maxim D. Shrayer, bilingual author, scholar, and translator, was born in Moscow in 1967 to a Jewish-Russian family with Ukrainian and Lithuanian roots and spent over eight years as a refusenik. He and his parents, the writer David Shrayer-Petrov ז״ל and the translator Emilia Shrayer, left the USSR and immigrated to the United States in 1987. Shrayer received a PhD from Yale University in 1995. He is Professor of Russian, English, and Jewish Studies at Boston College, where he cofounded the Jewish Studies Program. Shrayer has authored and edited thirty books of nonfiction, criticism, fiction, poetry, and translations. His poetry collections include the Russian-language *Tabun nad lugom* (*Herd above the Meadow*, New York, 1990), *Amerikanskii romans* (*American Romance*, Moscow, 1994), *N'iukheivenskie sonety* (*New Haven Sonnets*, Providence, 1998), *Stikhi iz aipada* (*Poems from the iPad*, Tel Aviv, 2022), and *Voina* (*War*, Tal Aviv, 2025), and the English-language *Of Politics and Pandemics* (Boston, 2020) and *Kinship* (Georgetown, KY, 2024). Among Shrayer's other books are the literary memoirs *Waiting for America*, *Leaving Russia*, and *Immigrant Baggage* and the collections *Yom Kippur in Amsterdam* and *A Russian Immigrant: Three Novellas*. He is the recipient of a number of awards and fellowships, including a 2007 National Jewish Book Award and a 2012 Guggenheim Fellowship. Shrayer's publications have been translated into thirteen languages, most recently *Nabokov e o Judaísmo*, published in Brazil in 2023, and *Immigrato russo*, published in Italy in 2024. He lives in Massachusetts with his wife, Dr. Karen E. Lasser, a medical editor, researcher, and physician; their daughters, Mira Isabella and Tatiana Rebecca; and their silver Jewdle, Stella.

The Jewish Poetry Project

jpoetry.us

Ben Yehuda Press

From the Coffee House of Jewish Dreamers: Poems of Wonder and Wandering and the Weekly Torah Portion by Isidore Century

"Isidore Century is a wonderful poet. His poems are funny, deeply observed, without pretension." —*The Jewish Week*

The House at the Center of the World: Poetic Midrash on Sacred Space by Abe Mezrich

"Direct and accessible, Mezrich's midrashic poems often tease profound meaning out of his chosen Torah texts. These poems remind us that our Creator is forgiving, that the spiritual and physical can inform one another, and that the supernatural can be carried into the everyday."
—Yehoshua November, author of *God's Optimism*

**we who desire:
Poems and Torah riffs by Sue Swartz**

"Sue Swartz does magnificent acrobatics with the Torah. She takes the English that's become staid and boring, and adds something that's new and strange and exciting. These are poems that leave a taste in your mouth, and you walk away from them thinking, what did I just read? Oh, yeah. It's the Bible."
—Matthue Roth, author, *Yom Kippur A Go-Go*

Open My Lips: Prayers and Poems by Rachel Barenblat

"Barenblat's God is a personal God—one who lets her cry on His shoulder, and who rocks her like a colicky baby. These poems bridge the gap between the ineffable and the human. This collection will bring comfort to those with a religion of their own, as well as those seeking a relationship with some kind of higher power."
—Satya Robyn, author, *The Most Beautiful Thing*

Words for Blessing the World: Poems in Hebrew and English by Herbert J. Levine

"These writings express a profoundly earth-based theology in a language that is clear and comprehensible. These are works to study and learn from."
—Rodger Kamenetz, author, *The Jew in the Lotus*

Shiva Moon: Poems by Maxine Silverman

"The poems, deeply felt, are spare, spoken in a quiet but compelling voice, as if we were listening in to her inner life. This book is a precious record of the transformation saying Kaddish can bring. It deserves to be read."
—Howard Schwartz, author, *The Library of Dreams*

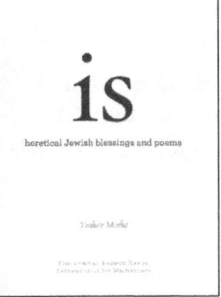

is: heretical Jewish blessings and poems by Yaakov Moshe (Jay Michaelson)

"Finally, Torah that speaks to and through the lives we are actually living: expanding the tent of holiness to embrace what has been cast out, elevating what has been kept down, advancing what has been held back, reveling in questions, revealing contradictions."
—Eden Pearlstein, aka eprhyme

Texts to the Holy: Poems
by Rachel Barenblat

"These poems are remarkable, radiating a love of God that is full bodied, innocent, raw, pulsating, hot, drunk. I can hardly fathom their faith but am grateful for the vistas they open. I will sit with them, and invite you to do the same."
—Merle Feld, author of *A Spiritual Life*

The Sabbath Bee: Love Songs to Shabbat
by Wilhelmina Gottschalk

"Torah, say our sages, has seventy faces. As these prose poems reveal, so too does Shabbat. Here we meet Shabbat as familiar housemate, as the child whose presence transforms a family, as a spreading tree, as an annoying friend who insists on being celebrated, as a woman, as a man, as a bee, as the ocean."
—Rachel Barenblat, author, *The Velveteen Rabbi's Haggadah*

All the Holes Line Up: Poems and Translations
by Zackary Sholem Berger

"Spare and precise, Berger's poems gaze unflinchingly at—but also celebrate—human imperfection in its many forms. And what a delight that Berger also includes in this collection a handful of his resonant translations of some of the great Yiddish poets."
—Yehoshua November, author of *God's Optimism* and *Two Worlds Exist*

How to Bless the New Moon:
Songs of the Sovereign and the Icon
by Rachel Kann

"Rachel Kann is a master wordsmith. Her poems are rich in content, packed with life's wisdom and imbued with soul. May this collection of her work enable more of the world to enjoy her offerings."
—Sarah Yehudit Schneider, author of *You Are What You Hate*

Into My Garden: Prayers
by David Caplan

"The beauty of Caplan's book is that it is not polemical. It does not set out to win an argument or ask you whether you've put your tefillin on today. These gentle poems invite the reader into one person's profound, ambiguous religious experience."
—*The Jewish Review of Books*

Between the Mountain and the Land is the Lesson: Poetic Midrash on Sacred Community by Abe Mezrich

"Abe Mezrich cuts straight back to the roots of the Midrashic tradition, sermonizing as a poet, rather than ideologue. Best of all, Abe knows how to ask questions and avoid the obvious answers."
—Jake Marmer, author, *Jazz Talmud*

NOKADDISH: Poems in the Void
by Hanoch Guy Kaner

"A subversive, midrashic play with meanings—specifically Jewish meanings, and then the reversal and negation of these meanings."
—Robert G. Margolis

An Added Soul: Poems for a New Old Religion
by Herbert J. Levine

"Herbert J. Levine's lovely poems swing wide the double doors of English and Hebrew and open on the awe of being. Clear and direct, at ease in both tongues, these lyrics embrace a holiness unyoked from myth and theistic searching."
—Lynn Levin, author, *The Minor Virtues*

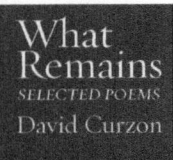

What Remains
by David Curzon

"Aphoristic, ekphrastic, and precise revelations animate WHAT REMAINS. In his stunning rewriting of Psalm 1 and other biblical passages, Curzon shows himself to be a fabricator, a collector, and an heir to the literature, arts, and wisdom traditions of the planet."
—Alicia Ostriker, author of *The Volcano and After*

The Shortest Skirt in Shul
by Sass Oron

"These poems exuberantly explore gender, Torah, the masks we wear, and the way our bodies (and the ways we wear them) at once threaten stable narratives, and offer the kind of liberation that saves our lives."
—Alicia Jo Rabins, author of *Divinity School*, composer of *Girls In Trouble*

Walking Triptychs
by Ilya Gutner

These are poems from when I walked about Shanghai and thought about the meaning of the Holocaust.

Book of Failed Salvation
by Julia Knobloch

"These beautiful poems express a tender longing for spiritual, physical, and emotional connection. They detail a life in movement—across distances, faith, love, and doubt."
—David Caplan, author, *Into My Garden*

Daily Blessings: Poems on Tractate Berakhot
by Hillel Broder

"Hillel Broder does not just write poetry about the Talmud; he also draws out the Talmud's poetry, finding lyricism amidst legality and re-setting the Talmud's rich images like precious gems in end-stopped lines of verse."
—Ilana Kurshan, author of *If All the Seas Were Ink*

The Red Door: A dark fairy tale told in poems
by Shawn C. Harris

"THE RED DOOR, like its poet author Shawn C. Harris, transcends genres and identities. It is an exploration in crossing worlds. It brings together poetry and story telling, imagery and life events, spirit and body, the real and the fantastic, Jewish past and Jewish present, to spin one tale." —Einat Wilf, author, *The War of Return*

The Missing Jew: Poems 1976-2022
by Rodger Kamenetz

"How does Rodger Kamenetz manage to have so singular a voice and at the same time precisely encapsulate the world view of an entire generation (also mine) of text-hungry American Jews born in the middle of the twentieth century?"
—Jacqueline Osherow, author, *Ultimatum from Paradise* and *My Lookalike at the Krishna Temple: Poems*

The Matter of Families
by Robert H. Deluty

"Robert Deluty's career-spanning collection of New and Selected poems captures the essence of his work: the power of love, joy, and connection, all tied together with the poet's glorious sense of humor. This book is Deluty's masterpiece."
—Richard M. Berlin, M.D., author of *Freud on My Couch*

There Is No Place Without You
by Maya Bernstein

"Bernstein's poems brim with energy and sound, moving the reader around a world mapped by motherhood, contemplation, religion, and the effects of illness on the body and spirit. Her language is lyrical, delicate, and poised; her lens is lucid and original."
—Anthony Anaxagorou, author of *After the Formalities*

Torah Limericks
by Rhonda Rosenheck

"Rhonda Rosenheck knows the Hebrew Bible, and she knows that it can stand up to the sometimes silly, sometimes snarky, but always insightful scholarship packed into each one of these interpretive jewels."
—Rabbi Hillel Norry

Words for a Dazzling Firmament
by Abe Mezrich

"Mezrich is a cultivated craftsman: interpretively astute, sonically deliberate, and spiritually cunning."

—Zohar Atkins, author of *Nineveh*

Everything Thaws
by R. B. Lemberg

"Full of glacier-sharp truths, and moments revealed between words like bodies beneath melting permafrost. As it becomes increasingly plain how deeply our world is shaped by war and climate change and grief and anger, articulating that shape feels urgent and necessary."
—Ruthanna Emrys, author of *A Half-Built Garden*

Ode to the Dove: *An illustrated, bilingual edition of a Yiddish poem by Abraham Sutzkever*
Zackary Sholem Berger, translator
Liora Ostroff, Illustrator

"An elegant volume for lovers of poetry."
—Justin Cammy, translator of *Sutzkever, From the Vilna Ghetto to Nuremberg: Memoir and Testimony*

Poems for a Cartoon Mouse
by Andrew Burt

"Andrew Burt's poetry magnifies the vanishingly small line between danger and safety. This collection asks whether order is an illusion that veils chaos, or vice-versa, juxtaposing images from the Bible with animated films."
—Ari Shapiro, host of NPR's *All Things Considered*

Old Shul
by Pinny Bulman

"Nostalgia gives way to a tender theology, a softly chuckling illumination from within the heart of/as a beautiful, broken sanctuary, somehow both gritty and fragile, grimy and iridescent – not unlike faith itself."
—Jake Marmer, author of *Cosmic Diaspora*

Feet In L.A., But My Womb Lives In Jerusalem, My Breath In Vermont
by Lori Levy

"Takes my breath away. With no pretense whatsoever, they leap, alive, from the page until this reader felt as if she were living Levy's life. How does the author do it?"
—Mary Jo Balistreri, author of *Still*

Poem Hashavuah
by Lexie Botzum and Jessica Spencer

"This collection illuminates the white fire of the Torah — the ancient and modern literary interpretations that carve out the negative space of the Torah's letters so that they dance before us as joyously as when they were given in fire on Sinai."
—Ilana Kurshan, author of *If All the Seas Were Ink*

Bits and Pieces
by Edward Pomerantz

"A natural dramatist who looks back on his life growing up in Washington Heights in a series of vivid vignettes inspired by his early moviegoing."
—Robert Vas Dias, author of *Poetics Of Still Life: A Collage*

Not Akhmatova
by Noah Berlatsky

"In these poems, Noah Berlatsky approaches the work of Anna Akhmatova—or scrambles off in another direction entirely. Writing under the sign of her name, with her but without trying to become her, Berlatsky gives us Anna in transcreation, in transelation."
—Sarah Dowling, author of *Entering Sappho*

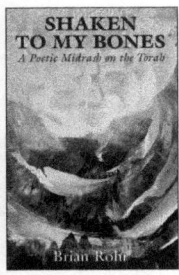

Shaken to My Bones
by Brian Rohr

"In Brian Rohr's exquisite poems, wonders unfold. We are taken along on a journey both ancient and immediate — one that is rewarding beyond comparison."
—Baruch November, author of *Bar Mitzvah Dreams*

So Many Warm Words: Selections from the Poetry of Rosa Nevadovska, translated by Merle L. Bachman

"This bilingual edition makes Nevadovska's oeuvre—poems of loneliness and longing countered by others expressing joyous moments of transcendence—accessible, for the first time, to the English reader."
—Sheva Zucker, editor emerita of *Afn Shvel*.

The Whole Mishpocha
by Philip Terman

"Gathers the Jewish-themed poems of an accomplished poet who has been producing memorable work on the Jewish-American experience for decades. I have long admired Terman's exceptional poems for their Jewish ethos, beautiful lyricism, and emotional risk taking."
—Yehoshua November, author of *God's Optimism*

Styx by Else Lasker-Schüler
translated by Mildred Faintly

"Reborn in Mildred Faintly's magnificent translation, Else Lasker-Schüler's STYX overflows with shudders of desolation, moans of sexual pleasure, ecstatic fusions of love and despite that exalt and torture in equal measure."
—Joy Ladin, author of *The Book of Anna* and *Shekhinah Speaks.*

Chrysalis Summer
by Suzanne Brody

"We are invited into the thoughts and emotions of one woman who plays many roles—teacher, mother, rabbi, and artist. Topics stretch from the mundane business of cleaning up students' glitter to weightier topics such as egalitarianism and Biblical texts."
—Dori Weinstein, author of the *YaYa & YoYo* series *Considered*

Blessed Are You, Wondrous Universe:
A Siddur for Seekers by Herbert J. Levine

"Herb Levine has fashioned a sparkling collection of prayers for a thinking, feeling modern person who wants to express gratitude for the wonder of existence."
—Daniel Matt, translator of the Zohar, author of *God and the Big Bang*, *The Essential Kabbalah*, and *Becoming Elijah*

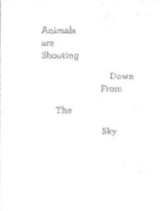

Animals are Shouting Down from the Sky
by Genevieve Greinetz

"Often heart-stopping, these poems abound in images uniquely unfamiliar. Not intended for the casual reader, they capture the violation of nature, free speech silenced, humanity flattened, families – and friends – failing as they often do."
—Merle Feld, author of *Longing, Poems for a Life*

www.ingramcontent.com/pod-product-compliance
Lightning Source LLC
LaVergne TN
LVHW041346080426
835512LV00006B/646